QED WHAT'S FOR LUNCH?

Meat and Fish

Honor Head

QED Publishing

Copyright © QED Publishing 2006

First published in the UK in 2006 by
QED Publishing
A Quarto Group company
226 City Road
London EC1V 2TT
www.qed-publishing.co.uk

A catalogue record for this book is available from the British Library.

ISBN 1 84538 476 8

Written by Honor Head
Designed by Danny Pyne
Edited by Hannah Ray and Barbara Bourassa
Consultancy by Roy Balam and Sarah Schenker of the British Nutrition Foundation
Photographer Michael Wicks
Illustrations by Bill Greenhead

Publisher Steve Evans
Art Director Zeta Davies
Editorial Director Jean Coppendale

Printed and bound in China

Picture credits
Key: t = top, b = bottom, c = centre, l = left, r = right, FC = front cover

Corbis/Amos Nachoum 19tr /Envision 21bl/photocuisine 21cl/
Macduff Everton 23cl/Paul Anton/Zefa 26b /Ronnie Kaufman 26c/
Tim Page 27c/Owen Franken 27t, b; **Ecoscene**/Peter Hulme 9m;
Getty Images/Allison Dinner 15tr/Gary John Norman 23tr/
SMader/ U Schmid 26t.

Before undertaking any activity which involves eating or the preparation of food,
always check whether the children in your care have any food allergies. In a classroom
situation, prior written permission from parents or guardians may be required.

Website information is correct at time of going to press. However, the publishers
cannot accept liability for any information or links found on third-party websites.

Words in **bold** can be found in the glossary on page 30.

Contents

Get balanced

To help keep your body healthy and happy, it is important to eat a balanced diet. But what exactly does this mean, and how can we make sure that our diet is balanced?

What is a balanced diet?

All foods can be put into one of five main groups:

fruit and vegetables

bread, other cereals and potatoes

milk and dairy foods

meat, fish and alternatives

foods that contain fats and sugars

A balanced diet means eating foods from all five groups. However, not all foods should be eaten in the same amounts. This plate shows how much of your diet should be made up from each of the groups.

What's in each group?

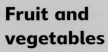

Bread, other cereals and potatoes

Foods such as bread, potatoes, breakfast cereals, noodles, oats and rice are all in this group.

Fruit and vegetables

This group includes all fresh, frozen, dried or canned fruits and vegetables, plus 100 per cent fruit or vegetable juices.

Milk and dairy foods

Milk, cheese and yoghurt are all included in this group.

Meat, fish and alternatives

This group includes beef, pork, chicken, fish and other seafood, plus meat alternatives such as tofu, nuts and eggs.

Foods with fat and sugar

Margarine, butter, oil and mayonnaise all appear in this group, as well as sweets, jam and puddings.

Why eat a balanced diet?

A balanced diet is important because no one food can provide all the **vitamins**, **minerals** and other things that your body needs to work properly. A mix of tasty foods from each group is what you need to stay in tip-top condition.

Weblink

Some countries, such as the USA and Australia, use a special food pyramid instead of a plate to explain a balanced diet. To find out more, visit www.mypyramid.gov/kids

Meet meat...

This book is all about meat and fish. Meat is important as part of a balanced diet. It contains iron, which gives us healthy blood and muscles, as well as other vitamins and minerals which we need to stay fit and well. You can eat meat in lots of ways, but which animals give us which meat?

CHICKEN:

Well, chicken of course!

Meat matters

Meat is a good source of **protein**. Protein is essential to build muscles and help growth. It also helps your body to heal when you've got a cut or a scratch.

However, try to avoid meat that has a lot of fat. Too much fat is bad for you. It can make you overweight and can cause heart problems when you get older.

Bite Size

If you don't eat meat or fish, you must get your protein from other sources. Eat protein-packed foods such as eggs, **soya**, nuts, seeds and pulses (these are peas, beans, chickpeas and lentils).

SHEEP:

Lamb

Mutton

Kofta kebabs

Mince

6

Q. When is meat not meat?
A. When it's tofu!

Tofu is a type of meat substitute that is made from a plant. It can be cooked in the same way as meat and contains loads of protein. Tofu can be eaten by vegetarians and is very low in fat. Give it a try!

COWS:

Beef

Steak

Beefburgers

Kebabs

Mince

PIGS:

Pork

Ham

Sausages

Salami

Bacon

CHECK IT OUT!

Red meat comes from cows, sheep and lambs. It is very red and looks dark when it is cooked. Pork is also red meat, but is a lighter colour.

White meat comes from **poultry**, such as chickens and turkeys. It looks light pink when it is raw and white once it has been cooked.

TURKEY:

Yes, you've guessed it – it's turkey!

Try it!

When choosing meat look for the word 'lean'. This means the meat does not have as much fat on it and is better for you.

Fish –
the fit food

From fishfingers to squid rings, fish is great for keeping your brain and body super fit. All fish taste different, so why not try a few and see which you like the best?

Which fish?

There are two types of fish – white fish and oily fish. White fish, such as cod, are low in fat. Oily fish contain special types of fats that can help keep us healthy. These fats are great for your brain, heart, bones and just about everything else you can think of! The top five oily fish are:

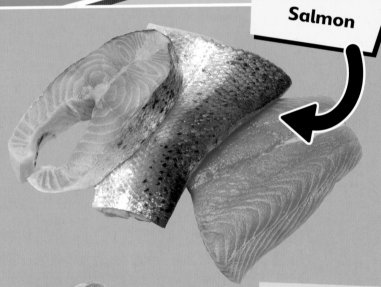

Salmon

Fresh tuna

Sardines

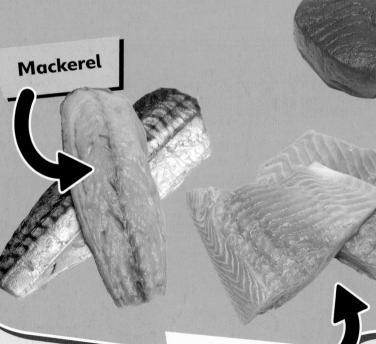

Mackerel

Trout

Point the finger

Fishfingers are a healthy lunch choice for the school canteen if they are made from good-quality fish. If fishfingers are on the school lunch menu, ask whether they were fried or grilled. Grilled fishfingers are much better for you.

This man is feeding the fish at a salmon farm.

CHECK IT OUT!

Most of the fish we buy at the supermarket has been caught at sea. However, some of the fish that we buy, such as trout or salmon, may have been farmed. This means a huge number of fish are kept in a small space. They are regularly treated with chemicals and **pesticides** to keep them healthy.

Organic fish are bred on a farm, but they are not fed **artificial** foods or sprayed with pesticides.

Weblink

Find out more about different types of fish and seafood at www.seafish-education.org.uk

Fish facts

For a really balanced and healthy diet, you should try to eat fish at least twice a week, one of which should be an oily fish.

Try it!

Fish and chips are very tasty but they contain a lot of fat and should only be enjoyed once in a while. Try oven-baked fish as a healthy alternative to fried fish.

Lunch choice

Ham sandwich

A ham sandwich makes a great packed lunch. It's tasty, it doesn't make the bread soggy and it doesn't dribble down your front when you eat it!

CHECK IT OUT!

Ham is a great lunchbox option but it is high in salt and can be fatty, so look out for reduced-salt or lean versions. Try to have a different filling in your sandwich every day.

Carton of fruit juice

Pear

Yoghurt

Cherry tomatoes

Ham it up!

Ham starts out as a roast leg of pork. The roast leg is salted to preserve it. At the shops you will see ham on the bone and **processed** in packets. Both are delicious in sandwiches or salads.

Get creative

What else could you add to ham to make the perfect jumbo-sized sandwich? Here are some ideas:

Try it!

If you buy ham that is freshly cut off the bone, trim off the fat before you eat it – super tasty and better for you.

Mustard

Cheese

More slices of bread!

Coleslaw

Cress

Ham sandwich in brown bread

Mushrooms

Get balanced

To make a ham sandwich a more balanced lunch, add some slices of tomato and cucumber. Alternatively, try a double-decker. That's a slice of bread, then cheese, a second slice of bread, a slice of ham, some salad and a final slice of bread. Have a piece of fruit for pudding and a fresh-fruit drink.

Sausages

Lots of people like sausages, whether they're sliced in a sandwich, with mashed potatoes and onion gravy or enjoyed for breakfast with eggs and beans, but what is a sausage?

How sausages are made...

(1)

(2)

(3)

First of all, the meat is minced. Sausages are usually made from pork or beef.

Breadcrumbs, **seasoning** and **preservatives** are then mixed into the minced meat to make sausage meat.

The sausage meat is then stuffed inside a skin, or casing, to make sausages. The skins were originally made from the intestines of animals, but now they are mostly man-made.

Try it!

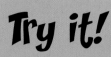

You can also buy vegetarian sausages made from tofu or vegetables. Why not try one?

Sausage shop

Most sausages have to be cooked before you can eat them. Pork and beef sausages can be fried, grilled or oven-cooked. Grilling is best as it gets rid of lots of fat. Cooked sausages can be eaten hot or cold (great in a lunchbox!).

Bite Size

The word sausage comes from the Latin *salsus*, which means salted or **preserved**. In the past, people did not have refrigerators to keep their meat cold, so they preserved it instead.

Cocktail sausages

These mini sausages make great party snacks.

Weblink

There are lots of different types of sausages from countries all over the world. To find out about some of them, visit www.foodsubs.com/MeatcureSausage.html

Frankfurter

Frankfurters can be eaten cold, or cooked and eaten in a roll as a hotdog.

STAR BUY!

Salami

Salami is made from dried, spicy meat and does not have to be cooked.

Low-fat sausage

These are very similar to pork sausages, but are lower in fat.

Pork sausage

Great with mash, these are one of the most common types of sausage.

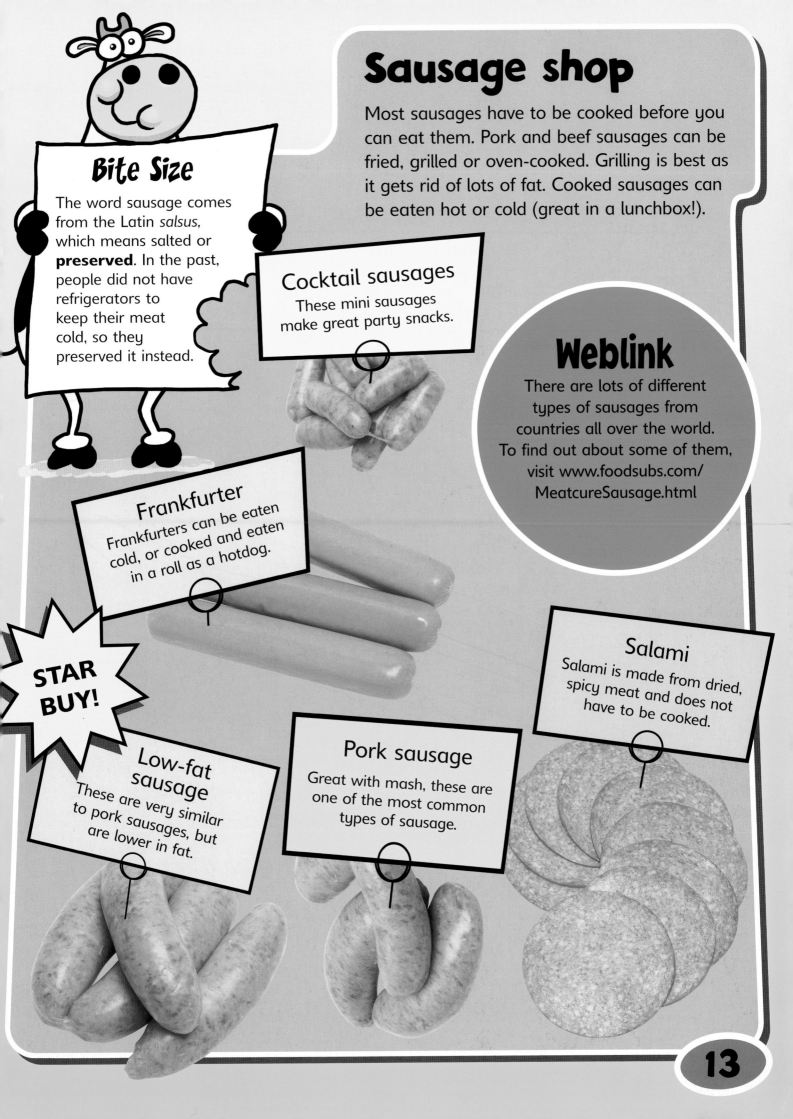

13

Lunch choice

Meat samosas

Samosas first came from India. These tasty triangular parcels, filled with meat or vegetables, are perfect for a lunchbox.

Fruit salad

How a samosa is made...

Mixed salad

Samosa pastry is made using **ghee**, flour and salt. The filling, often minced lamb, is gently fried in ghee or butter.

The samosa pastry is cut into triangles and a spoonful of filling is added to each one. The corners of the triangles are then folded in to make a parcel.

The samosas can be deep fried or baked in the oven. Baking them is healthier.

14

Top marks

To make a balanced lunch, try a meat samosa with a mixed salad and a small tub of rice with peas and diced, cooked vegetables. Have a couple of pieces of fruit or a fruit salad for dessert.

CHECK IT OUT!

An empanada is a Latin American version of the samosa. It can be filled with seafood, meat, cheese, vegetables or fruit. The name comes from the word *empanar*, which means to coat with bread.

Small tub of rice

Meat samosa

Fillings – no, not your teeth!

Samosas filled with spicy stewed apple make a delicious dessert. You could also try a berry filling, such as blackberries, strawberries, and raspberries, for a fruity lunchbox pudding.

Bite Size

If you're making your own samosas, you can use ready-made **filo pastry** instead of samosa pastry.

Hot 'n' spicy

Meat tastes great when cooked with spices or chillies. A bit messy for a lunchbox, but you never know what you might find on offer at the school canteen!

YUMMY CURRY

Curry is the Indian word for sauce, and that's what most curries are – meat or vegetables cooked in a spicy sauce. Chillies can be added to make a really hot sauce but you can also get mild curries, which are very tasty and not hot at all.

THE GOOD CURRY GUIDE

Try to choose a curry with a tomato-based sauce rather than a cream-based sauce. They are better for you.

•

You could also try curries that contain lentils and other vegetables as a change to meat.

•

Choose plain, boiled rice, or try brown rice for a change.

•

For a really 'good-for-you' curry, have a side salad, too.

Weblink

Chapattis are Indian flatbreads that are often used to scoop up curry. To find out how to make your own, visit www.bbc.co.uk/food/recipes/database/chapatis_77146.shtml

Say 'hi' to a Thai

Thailand is another place that is famous for its curries. They are hot and spicy, like Indian curries, but usually have creamier sauces. Many Thai curries are made with coconut milk or creamed coconut. Coconut milk is low in fat, but creamed coconut contains much more fat, so curries made from this should be kept as a treat!

Fresh coconut

Coconut milk

Block of creamed coconut

Make mine Mexican

Many spicy Mexican dishes contain meat or fish. Any meat can be served rolled up in a tortilla, which is a flatbread made from wheat flour or ground corn. Another popular dish is made using tamales, or corn husks, filled with chicken or pork. Many Mexican dishes are topped with a spicy salsa. This is a hot sauce made from tomatoes. And if you like your food super-hot, you can always add a few chillies!

Try it!

If you eat ready-made curries, check the label to see how much fat and salt they contain. Try making your own at home – delicious and good for you!

Lunch choice

Tuna salad

Tuna salad is a tasty lunch option. It's delicious, good for you and you can throw in anything that you fancy – within reason!

Let's talk tuna

Tuna comes from the tuna fish – no surprises there! It is easy to prepare as it can be taken straight from the can and used in salads, sandwiches, pitta pockets or with jacket potatoes. In cans, it comes in brine (salty water), oil or spring water. Spring water is a very healthy choice, so look out for it. If you prefer one of the others, make sure all the liquid is drained off before eating the tuna.

Bottle of water

Fruit salad

Tuna salad with low-fat mayonnaise

Dip in

Here's a great, speedy recipe for a fun school lunch or snack.

Yum!

1 Mix a can of tuna with low-fat mayonnaise or yoghurt to make a smooth paste.

2 Add some sweetcorn, chopped spring onion or any of your favourite things.

Tuna mix

Tuna mixes well with loads of things. Here are some suggestions for salads and sandwich fillings, but why not experiment with your own choices as well?

This is what tuna look like in the sea. Tuna fish travel in huge groups called shoals.

Cooked peas

Sweetcorn

Red or green pepper

Spring onions

Cucumber

Celery

Tub of rice pudding

Brown bread roll

CHECK IT OUT!

A few years ago, fishermen used to catch tuna by chasing dolphins and dropping big nets over the huge shoals of tuna that follow dolphins around. However, millions of dolphins were killed by the nets. Now there are dolphin-friendly ways to catch tuna. Look out for the special 'dolphin friendly' labels on cans of tuna.

3 Flavour with pepper and eat as a dip with nachos, pitta fingers or carrot sticks.

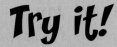

Try it!

When making a tuna dip or salad, try using low-fat mayonnaise or yoghurt. If you use full-fat mayonnaise, try not to use too much.

19

Fishy things

Fish comes in cans, smoked, **filleted** and as a paste. It also comes as fishfingers, but how do we get from a fish to a fishfinger?

How fishfingers are made...

1 The fish, usually cod, are filleted and skinned. The fillets are frozen into large blocks. The blocks are then cut into fishfinger shapes.

2 The fingers are covered in batter and sprinkled with breadcrumbs.

3 The fishfingers are flash fried. They are fried so quickly that the fish stays frozen.

4 Then the fingers are packed. They come out frozen, boxed and ready to load onto the lorries for the shops.

A fish called hoki is also used to make fish fingers. This is to protect the numbers of cod that are left in the oceans.

Rainbow trout
Rainbow trout live in freshwater lakes and streams. They get their name from the bright colours of their skin.

Salmon
Salmon can be grilled, oven-baked or smoked. It contains lots of healthy oils.

Crab
There are many different types of crab that can be eaten. Soft crab meat can be found inside the hard shell.

Mussels
Mussels are a type of shellfish. Once it is cooked, you have to take the mussel out of its shell before you can eat it.

Plaice
Plaice are flatfish. The white meat of this fish is often filleted, coated in breadcrumbs or batter and fried.

Snapper
This brightly coloured fish has white meat and tastes great when cooked on a barbecue.

Prawns
Cooked prawns are often eaten cold as part of a prawn cocktail with lettuce and a special sauce.

Lunch choice

Chicken Pitta

Chicken is a great choice for a lunchbox – easy to eat, tasty and very good for you.

Red kidney beans

Chopped peppers

Chicken – the perfect fowl

Chicken is almost too good to be true! Not only does it taste delicious both hot or cold, it can be cooked in almost any way you can think of and goes well with loads of other foods. It is full of protein and low in fat (as long as you remove the skin!). Chicken is perfect for a lunchbox. Have it in a pitta with a choice of fillings, or in a sandwich or a roll. Here are some ideas for lovely lunchboxes:

PITTAS

- Chicken, rice and sweetcorn
- Chicken, chopped walnuts and green grapes
- Cold chicken tikka with green salad
- Chicken with mayonnaise, raisins or currants and nuts
- Chicken with potato salad
- Chicken with pasta

SANDWICHES

- Layered sandwich with ham and chicken
- Chicken and cheese with pickle
- Chicken with salsa
- Chicken with coleslaw
- Chicken with tomato slices and rings of raw onion
- Chicken with prawns in low-fat mayonnaise

Is free-range the same as organic?

Most chickens are factory farmed. This means they are kept in small cages and fed food which has been mixed with **additives** to make them bigger. Free-range chickens are allowed to wander around freely. Organic chickens roam freely as well, and eat only natural food.

▲ Factory-farmed chickens

◄ Free-range chickens

Brown pitta pocket

Chicken pieces

Chicken choice

Fed up with sandwiches? Try making your own chicken kebabs. Thread some chicken cubes onto small kebab sticks. Grill or oven bake, then eat with a honey and mustard dip. Keep a tissue handy for drips!

Turkey talk

Turkey is another healthy food and can be eaten in the same way as chicken. For super-healthy turkey, don't have too much stuffing!

Try it!

There is one naughty bit about chicken and that's the skin. Just under the skin is where the fat can be found. Throw away the skin and enjoy the rest.

The burger bar

Okay, so you've heard all the bad news about burgers, but are they really as bad for you as the grown-ups say?

Burger baddies?

Not all burgers are made from 100 per cent beef. If you're a real burger addict, why not try making your own? It's fun and they can be much better for you than shop-bought burgers. For a healthy and ultra-tasty lunchbox special, try a home-made burger in a brown pitta pocket with salad.

Weblink

For fun and easy-to-make burger recipes, go to www.zip4tweens.com. Click on 'Recipes' then 'Around-The-World Mini Burgers'.

Burn off a burger

To burn off the **calories** gained by eating a large burger, you would need to do 105 minutes of swimming, 132 minutes of jogging or 176 minutes of walking!

Bite Size

Hamburgers are traditionally made from beef. They are called hamburgers after the city of Hamburg in Germany, but no one really knows where hamburgers came from originally.

Top toppings

You can add all sorts of tasty toppings to your burger. How about these?

Pickled gherkins

Ketchup

Low-fat mayonnaise

Tomato slices

Best burgers

Vegetarian burgers are a tasty and healthy alternative if you don't eat meat, and beanburgers will make you full of, well, beans! Try a veggie burger next time they're on the school lunch menu or eat them at home with vegetables and oven-baked chips for a healthy meal that's top of the class!

Veggie burger

Cauliflower, beans and carrots

Oven-baked chips

Pinboard

Check out the pinboard to see how meat is eaten in different ways around the world.

Mexico

In Mexico, people eat a dish called enchilada. These are tortillas filled with meat and beans and then baked in the oven.

France

The French enjoy eating pâté with crusty bread.

USA

In the USA, it is traditional for families to have a turkey dinner at Thanksgiving.

Italy

Some countries, such as Italy, have a special dried sausage called salami, which is eaten in slices.

Portugal

In Portugal, fresh sardines are grilled on barbecues on the beach.

Malaysia

In Malaysia, they eat satay. Satay are spicy mini kebabs made from chicken or beef and served with a peanut sauce.

Quiz time

Multiple-choice

1. Eating a balanced diet is important because:
a. it keeps your body healthy
b. it helps you fight off illness
c. it helps you to grow
d. all of the above

2. Which of these toppings tastes good in a ham sandwich?
a. mustard
b. cheese
c. ice cream
d. all of the above

3. Which of the following types of sausage is lowest in fat?
a. frankfurter
b. pork sausage
c. low-fat sausage
d. salami

4. Which is the healthiest choice on this list?
a. fried samosa
b. baked empanada
c. cream-based curry
d. Thai curry made with creamed coconut

5. Which vegetables go well with tuna fish?
a. spring onion
b. sweetcorn
c. celery
d. all of the above

Match the food with its food group

Dairy foods

Bread and cereals

Fats and sugars

Fruit and vegetables

Meat, fish and alternatives

True or false?

1. Salmon is not a healthy fish choice.
2. Crabs live in ponds.
3. Chicken is high in fat.
4. Tomato is a healthy topping for hamburgers.
5. Veggie burgers taste bad.
6. The French have Thanksgiving dinner with turkey.
7. In Portugal, fresh sardines are grilled on the beach.
8. Vitamins help us to stay healthy.
9. Ham comes from chickens.
10. Tofu is low in fat.

What's the answer?

1. From which food groups should you eat the most food?
2. Is baking food better than frying it?
3. What do vegetarians eat instead of meat?
4. Can you find out about some meat dishes from around the world that are not in this book?
5. What different things could you have in your lunchbox for a week to help you eat a balanced diet?

Answers

True or false?
1. FALSE
2. FALSE
3. FALSE
4. TRUE
5. FALSE
6. FALSE
7. TRUE
8. TRUE
9. FALSE
10. TRUE

What's the answer?
There is not necessarily a right or a wrong answer to these questions, so discuss your answers with your teacher or a parent.

Multiple choice
1. d – all of the above
2. a and b – mustard and cheese
3. c – low-fat sausage
4. b – baked empanada
5. d – all of the above

Match the food to its food group
Cheese – Dairy foods
Strawberries – Fruit and vegetables
Sardines – Meat, fish and alternatives
Bread – Bread and cereals
Chocolate cake – Fats and sugar

Glossary

additives Added ingredients such as colourings, that are not found in the food in its natural state

artificial Something that is not natural, but man-made

calories Units of energy found in all foods

filleted When all the bones have been removed from fish or chicken

filo pastry A type of thin pastry

ghee Butter that has been melted slowly to separate out the golden oil from the milk parts

mince Meat which has been chopped or ground into tiny pieces

minerals Natural substances found in food that help to keep our bodies healthy. For example, calcium, which helps strengthen bones and teeth

pesticides Chemicals that are sprayed onto growing food to keep pests or insects away

poultry Birds such as chickens and turkeys

preservatives Ingredients added to certain foods so that they last longer

preserve To do something to food (for example, pickle it or salt it) so that it lasts longer

processed When a food has been through a series of actions to make it look different from its natural state

protein Part of the food we eat which helps to build muscles and keep us healthy

seasoning Salt, pepper and similar ingredients that are added to food to improve the flavour

soya A vegetarian food made from the soya bean

vitamins Substances found in the food we eat that are needed to help us to stay healthy

Index

Parents' and teachers' notes

- Before you read the book, have a general discussion about food. Talk about favourite foods. Which is the classroom favourite, what do the children class as 'good foods' and what do they consider 'bad foods'? Why? Do the children care about what they eat? Why?

- Talk about what the children plan to eat for lunch today, or what they have already had for lunch. Did they enjoy it? Did they think they had a healthy lunch? How could it have been healthier?

- Look at the 'Lunch choice' photographs in the book. Can the children identify the different food groups in each picture? Which are their favourites, and why? How would they make each food choice better?

- Has reading the book changed the children's minds about any foods? If so, why?

- Discuss the meat choices available for school lunches in the school canteen. Do the children think the choices are tasty or healthy? Do they have a favourite?

- Cut out pictures of meals from magazines and restaurant promotions. Stick them on the wall. Discuss the best meals in terms of taste and health. Look at the meat content. Is it a healthy option? How could it be improved?